C0-ASY-086

COLUMBIA COLLEGE LIBRARY

DO TELL SOMEONE!

Inner Turmoils Surrounding Sexual Abuse Victims

DISCARD

BY YVONNIA HOUSTON

Grateful acknowledgement is made to the following publishers and authors for permission to reprint:

Excerpt from OPRAH! by Robert Waldron
Copyright © 1987 by Robert Waldron
Reprinted by permission of St. Martin's Press, Inc., New York

Excerpt from WHEN RABBIT HOWLS by Trudy Chase
Copyright © 1987 by Trudi Chase
Reprinted by permission of the publisher, Dutton, an imprint of New American Library, a division of Penguin Books USA, Inc.

DO TELL SOMEONE!
Copyright ©1991 by Yvonnia Houston
All rights reserved, no part of this book may be reproduced in any form without written permission from the publisher, except by a reviewer who wishes to quote briefly in connection with a review in a magazine or a newspaper. For information, please write: SHANE PUBLICATIONS, P.O. Box 3873, San Rafael, California 94912-3873

First Edition

LIBRARY OF CONGRESS CATALOGING IN PUBLICATION DATA

International Standard Book Number   0-9628235-0-3
Library of Congress Catalog #90-84068   *CIP*

```
364.153 H843d

Houston, Yvonnia.

Do tell someone!
```

FOREWORD

Sexual abuse has been occuring for many years. No one is immune to it. Each incident has a devastating effect, leaving behind a wide variety of emotions. Fear, shame and anger are a few of the more common examples. It reduces self-esteem in such a way that even the most confident person can't escape its horrors. It can also cause confusion, depression, suicidal tendencies, insanity and emotional turmoil that can last for many years. Many victims, when left untreated become victims many times again. Some turn to prostitution, gigolos, mental institutions, residents of penal institutions, residents of drug and alcohol abuse centers etc. These are the ones you hear about most often and wonder why they chose to lead these type of life styles. These victims have these problems without consciously knowing it stems from their unfortunate past of having been sexually abused. Other victims that you don't hear or know so much about go on to become dysfunctional, possibly abusive parents who perpetuate the same kind of behavior by allowing their own children to be victimized, or victimizing their children in the same manner.

One way to deal with this problem is prevention. You can't ever start too early teaching your children to recognize potential harm. Teach them about "good touches" and "bad touches" with extra emphasis on telling parents or any trusted adult if ever an uncomfortable touch does occur. Please believe your child when he\she comes to you and take measures to solve the problem. Children don't lie about "bad touches". It may take a while for the child to gain the courage to reveal when a "bad touch" has occurred and when they do, intervention need to take place immediately.

There are many people in a trusted position to whom your child can fall victim. Some of whom are the father, stepfather, uncle, clergy, brother, mother, stepmother, grandfather, other distant relatives, friends of parents, their own friends, teachers, baby sitters, dates and neighbors just to name a few. There are others that are strangers, but more often the victim knows and trusts their assailant so be aware.

The best way to deal with this type of crime is to seek professional and legal help. In this manner the victim will be able to identify the problem and work on it before they get out of control.

Teach your child self-confidence and foster it regularly. Help them develop and maintain a healthy, strong self-esteem. If they fall victim to such tragedy in their life help them to restore that self-esteem.

Loretta Leach, R.N.

THANKS

To God for blessing me with a piece of your creativity
to write this book in the manner that I have.

To the entire staff at the Civic Center Library in Marin county
for your endless help during my research and for your valuable
hard work in the upkeep of resource materials.

To mother Verlean Houston for keeping an open eye and ears
on pertinent information that helped form this book and for
many years of support.

To Jurlene Scruggs for unlimited "typing patience", loving
guidance and words of wisdom over the years.

To Stennis Scruggs for your enduring patience throughout
computer lessons and for providing an extra boost of needed
faith.

To Ruth Rockie Williams for your burst of positive energy that
assured "you can do it!"

To the one and only Ann Landers whose therapeutic column I
shall always be grateful for.

To Kathy Robinson for being supportive and a very dear friend.

To all of my teachers from kindergarten through college for
teaching me.

Especially to Mrs. Joan Cone for making writing fun and for
reading poetry aloud which inspired me to start writing in
such a manner.

Especially to Mr. Bob Doerr who encouraged me to change my
major to writing and for seeing the potential when I didn't.

To son Jamie for your patience which sometimes meant neglect
on my part during "writing hours".

To Michael for your love, support and most of all your ears for
listening.

Table of Contents

To my children
Jamie, Le Juan & Michael
May God bless you always

This book is dedicated to all

SURVIVORS!!

CRUEL

I left home very young because things just weren't right
Instances of him in my bed when you were sleep at night
I did tell but "oh no!" you said "that I can't believe"
"My husband isn't capable of such, from here you must leave"

So out I went into the world not knowing what was for me
To do at such an early age but, at least was free
Little did I know that there were others just as cruel
Who'd take advantage of me too and make me out their fool

More hurt, more pain, and more unhappiness I did endure
With this little heart of mine that once was free and pure
Things were so bad I did not know which way to turn or go
Or even if there was a reason for my existing so

Then one day I stumbled in the greatest building on earth
And discovered after all love in the universe
As I listened I realized that God is very kind
He has truly given me back my peace of mind

SEXUAL ABUSES

Mom knew dad was sleeping with me, she just turned her head
She didn't do a thing about him climbing in my bed
"He is a drunk, he don't know better" were some of the excuses
While my precious body ached his sexual abuses

She said she didn't want bad publicity
Never mind the hell that he was causing me
Her only concern was our neighbors' thoughts
She didn't even try to bring it to a halt

After several years, no more could I take
I had to go for my sanity's sake
I am far away from both my parents now
I thank the Lord that I made it through somehow

KIDNAP RAPE

Pretending to solicit
money for a church donation
Instead he kidnapped me
for sexual exploitation

I was told that my parents
no longer wanted me
He said to him they had
relinquished custody

For seven years
I was sexually abused
He said call him dad
mind was so confused

Mature, he lost interest in me
and kidnapped more young prey
When he went to work
we both ran away

I didn't want him to
go through what I had
Police turned us back over
to our mom and dad

At first I did not
recognize my father
But was glad to be back
home with him and mother

ARRANGED RAPE

My mother allowed me to be abused
By a man that she owed drug money to
She told me to pretend that I was a runaway
What she'd actually done was arranged the rape

In the apartment of a convicted rapist she left me alone
Who in turn raped me while she was gone
I was hysterical when she came back
Uncaring she took me home and left to smoke more crack

After months of keeping it in, I finally told my father
He called the police who came and arrested her
I hate her guts and hope never to see her again
I pray to God one day that this nightmare will end

RAPING DRUNK

Four years ago I was raped
by my aunt's drunk boyfriend
That no good dirty dog
has struck again

He raped my little cousin
who's only ten years old
But our family did not
believe her when she told

They didn't believe me either
when I told what he'd did
Said I just wanted attention
and was being a silly kid

I still have bad nightmares
can't stand the sight of him
I feel really bad that my
cousin is his latest victim

I feel a sense of duty
to let someone know
Since our kin won't help
where else can I go?

DEGRADED

My step-dad stopped
sleeping with mom in bed
When she went to work
he slept with me instead

He fondled all over
me and my baby brother
Said if I told he'd kill us
that included mother

Fondling led to rape
sodomy, oral copulation
Inside I felt
human degradation

I shot him in his back
real good one day
Time came to press charges
not one word would he say

PAINFUL SECRET

My own father has slept with me in bed
"It is a part of growing" is all he ever said
Seem he never wanted to lay when mom was there
He said it was our secret and that she wouldn't care

It was very painful when he laid me down
"You will get used to it" as he sexed me like a hound
I tried my very best to hold back the cry
But inside it felt as if I were going to die

It seemed from this bondage I'd never be free
As years went by he just kept prying into me
I finally grew the nerve to say I'd take no more
No longer would I be treated as my daddy's whore

That day "our secret" came to a stop
It was no longer possible to view him as my pop
When I go to sleep I have real bad dreams
The pain will always be, that's how it seems

INSANE RAPIST!

Committed at seven to
a mental institute
Because dad treated me
like a prostitute

It started when mom
left me in his care
In a hotel room
he made me strip bare

He tied up my arm
shot drugs in my vein
Did things to me
he knew were insane

Reunited with mom
two years later I told
I had to rid my chest
of that heavy load

I'm very young
and totally confused
With so many women out there
daddy there's no excuse!

ONLY THIRTEEN

*I was only thirteen
when I had my first baby
A cousin over twice my age
treated me like a lady*

*To our relatives
he blatantly denied
She's his spitting image
it's obvious he lied*

*My sister said he should've been
put under the jail to rot
My daughter is very beautiful
and everyone loves her a lot*

FORCEFULLY ENTERED

Teacher said stay after school
for extra help with my study
When everyone was gone
he forcefully entered my body

No one believed me
when I told what he'd done
They stayed away from me
our friendship was disowned

His wife, bless her heart came forth
said he was guilty indeed
She said he'd raped another in
the town where they'd lived previously

MOLEST TEACHER

Molested by my teacher
when I was in grade three
I told but
no one believed me

I lost interest in school
drifted one grade to the next
Eventually I gave up
and threw away my text

I fell in love with a guy
who said he'd protect me
Only thing he did was
put me on the street

My self-esteem plunged
to an all time low
At fifteen years of age
I became a hoe

Later I found out
the teacher did confess
Too bad they didn't listen
when I was at my best

SODOMIZED

"Be aware" my sisters
mom always warned
I her son was not told
of perverts to be alarmed

Right under her nose
the neighbor sodomized me
He said it was a secret
between him and me

One day we were riding
I burst into tears
And told how he hurt me
badly in my rear

SICK JOYS

Let us not forget
to warn our little boys
About the sex maniacs
who seek them for sick joys

FORCED OPEN

Mom was nice enough
to take in our cousin
A nice young man though
he definitely wasn't

I was in fourth grade when he
sneaked in my bed one night
And forced open my womb
with all of his might

I was so frightened
to tell what he'd done
He said it was just
a little game of fun

Thinking of it makes me feel
like a two bit slut
Today spaced out on drugs
to anybody I give it up

BITTEN PEE PEE

*My pee pee he used
to suck and bite
Somehow I felt
it was not right*

*Nobody paid me
any attention
When I decided
it to mention*

*Who will protect
the little one?
When this foul
thing is done*

DEADLY MOLEST

At four months old
I was laid to rest
Daddy molestation
was my cause of death

Molesting me, he pillowed my face
to stifle my cries
Unable to breathe
I shut my eyes

If this is but a sampling
the life I would've lived
I'm much better here
God please forgive

RAPE SALES

My sister, I and neighbor kids
were lined up for sex
By both of our mothers
so they could get a fix

Raped and molested three years
several times a week
johns picked among us
as if we were beef

While being raped
our moms just sat and looked
Their excuse for doing this
is that they were hooked

SEXUALLY MUTILATED

Lured into the woods
by his scare tact threats
At seven I was sexually
mutilated near death

Raped anal and orally
my penis was also chopped
Just because on him
I couldn't pee on top

He choked me with a cord
stabbed and left me to die
I was found bloody, naked
in the mud barely alive

Practically incoherent
when found after the attack
Unfortunately not soon enough to have
my genitals reattached

He was found guilty
in the first degree
I don't feel that I
will ever be set free

SORTED RAPIST

I had a big brother
who played lots of sports
I discovered he also liked
sex in different sorts

When our parents were gone
he slept with sisters and brothers
Promised us cookies and candy
if we didn't tell mother

I started having problems
mom begged me "what's wrong?"
It was hard to tell her
what he did when she was gone

One day she sent me
to a psychiatrist
I couldn't tell him either
something as awful as this

Years went by, I held in
all of the disgust
I didn't feel in anyone
I could ever trust

FRIGHTENED

Though it was beyond dark
Mom told me go play in the park
While she and her friends sat and smoke
Something I believe referred to as coke

This guy looked me up and down
Frightened, I tried to get around
He forced me down in the dirt
Pulled down my pants my "tee tee" was hurt

I rushed home and told my mother
Who still didn't wish to be bothered
I ran in my room and went to bed
Not another word about it was said

SCULPTURING RAPIST!

Daddy slept with both
my two sisters and I
Mom was fully aware
but chose to let it slide

Sculpturing wood
he stayed home all day
He'd become enraged if we
came home a minute late

"Be nice and I won't
meddle with your siblings"
He raped them both behind my back
until they were trembling

When he wanted me
he sent them to the store
He'd be finished when they
walked back through the door

One day there was a lecture
at school about sex abuse
Which informed to tell
if we were being used

We all came forth and
told what was going on
Both our parents
quickly left our home

TORE APART

I was very smart and
made good grades in school
Until mind cluttered of
being raped by that fool

It happened one day
when mom left me alone
With her boyfriend in the
few moments she was gone

As I cleaned my room
he came in and said
Come let me help you
clean up first your bed

He sneaked from behind
when I threw up the cover
Yanked me into bed
as if I were his lover

I shouted, kicked and screamed
he said no one will hear
Forced down my undies
and tore apart my rear

To mother he said he
really meant a lot
And if I cared for her
I'd say a thing not

TRICKED

At twelve years old
I ran away from home
Because daddy wouldn't
leave my body alone

Met at the bus station
by a real nice guy
Who treated me to dinner
and some cherry pie

When we finished eating
he showed me the town
I was very happy
as we drove around

One week later he said
"I need money quick"
To keep us going
I'd have to pull some tricks

Most johns said they
loved the younger girls
Said it was the best
feeling in the world

If daddy had kept his
filthy hands off me
I wouldn't be out here
on these ragged streets

DEVASTATED

My date said get ready we're going to the drive-in
We turned the corner in hopped his two friends
Forced to perform sex on all three of the scums
Totally devastated, they were just having fun

They laughed and laughed the entire while
I couldn't find a thing about to smile
Original date asked "well what's wrong?"
As he kindly drove me back home

When word circulated I felt so filthy
Despite them bastards were the ones guilty
I was so ashamed that I never did tell
Just suffered alone in my own hell

DADDY'S GIRL

Me and dad are parents
of a newborn
Though she is innocent
inside I still mourn

It's got to be the hardest
thing in all the world
For any daughter to birth
her own daddy's girl

What will I tell her
when gramp question comes?
She'll be so confused
when she learns they are one

Oh how I wish
things were different
between daddy and me

Oh how I wish
he would have
let my body be

FATHER'S SIN

*With help from the underground
me and my son are on the run
Because his own father used to
pry into his small rectum*

*We tried getting help
from the judicial system
They said he was fantasizing
and did not believe him*

*We miss our home
friends and family
But my main concern
is for his safety*

*It's so nice to see him
smiling once again
I hope one day he's able to
forget his father's sin*

VISIBLE RAPE

Four people passed
while I was being raped
On the ground near
Oakland's Merritt Lake

Struck by a man who
appeared out of thin air
He drug me down a slope
and tore off my underwear

Raped and beat ten minutes
while joggers continued to run
He told each one of them
that he had a gun

After the ordeal I drove
back to my Berkeley home
Badly bleeding and swelling
police were telephoned

They told me that I was
lucky to be alive
That no one called for help
they couldn't figure out why

PERVERTS

I'm three years old
I've contracted v.d.
My mom and her boyfriend
both laid up with me

She took me to the doctor
it was he who realized
That I'd been infected
police were notified

Mom told them she was
trying out masturbation
Her boyfriend said that he'd
performed oral copulation

I'm too young to know
exactly which words to use
To describe in detail
the perverted abuse

FORCIBLY RAMMED

One day my aunt gave
a big barbecue
I had to use it
when we were through

My cousin said I'll show you
the way to the bathroom
Once there he threw me inside
and forced off my blooms

He covered my mouth
with his oversized hands
My tee tee was broken
and forcibly rammed

"Don't ever tell anyone!"
he said
"If you do
you will end up dead"

He went back outside
as if nothing happened
Joined in with our
other relatives laughing

Painfully I made
my way out the door
But I never told
what happened to me at four

DISGRACE

When I was
six years of age
I experienced
a violent sex rage

While we were visiting
my great auntie
My decrepited uncle
peed inside me

I ran out of
the bathroom quick
Told mom in me
he put his stick

She held me tight
packed us in the car
From these relatives
we've stayed far

The incident effected
me a great deal
The very thought
of it makes me ill

With plenty of sex
all over the place
No one nowhere
should suffer this disgrace

SEXUALLY BLUDGEONED

Twenty years ago
dad killed my best friend
He sexually molested and
bludgeoned her head in

He said if I told
he would kill me too
"You'll be put away
and they won't believe you"

I forgot about it
after such a long time
One day it suddenly
all came back to mind

The only way I could
set my conscious free
Is by telling what I knew
to the authorities

My dear friend who was
only eight years old
Peace, love and may our
dear Lord bless her soul

STOLEN VIRGINITY

My precious little baby
was only three
When her daddy stole away
her virginity

I couldn't handle it
when I found out
So I took my little precious
and we both got out

Now we are fighting
whose custody she should be in
I know he just want her
so he can do it all again

DATE RAPE

My first sex encounter unfortunately was rape
By a friend who came for a dinner date
In the midst of eating he said come lets dance
Abruptly he threw me and tore off my pants

I tried everything I could to get him to stop
He ignored me and climbed right on top
I was very angry at having been betrayed
He acted as if everything was o.k.

Causally he said "well how was I?"
This despite tears coming down my eyes
I yelled at him to get out of my home
The whole rotten experience won't leave me alone

STAR RAPIST

*Because he was star of
the school's football team
I was urged "not to tell"
and destroy his dream*

*"Think of his reputation
along with bad publicity"
They didn't even address
the rotten things he did to me*

*It happened after we came
from a school gathering
He asked if he could come in
and have something to drink*

*He turned the music on
and up very loud
He then raped me but
no one heard me shout*

TWO BIT RAPIST

Like some two bit junkie
he had to have a fix
But instead of drugs
he fiend oral sex

He told my brother and I
not to tell our mom
That he made us lick him
when he baby sat in our home

HELPLESS

Of some baby sitters you must be aware
B-e-f-o-r-e leaving children in their care
They may not at all be what they appear
It's the normal look behind doors that turn queer

By my baby sitter I was repeatedly raped
Afraid to tell mom there seemed no escape
He rammed inside my body as though it were a toy
I felt very helpless as a little boy

He told me if I ever told mom
She would suffer bodily harm
That's why I kept the secret all shut up
That's why my life has been very corrupt

TRAUMATIZED

Dressed as a police he forced me in his car
While another drove us into woods afar
In all were six uniformed white men
Who raped and sodomized me over and over again

This pain and torture went on for days
My mouth is where their semen was sprayed
They scripted "kkk" on my upper torso
Also "nigger nigger" words were written just below

In a hefty garbage bag on the ground I lie
That is where they tossed me out to die
Found with stinky feces smeared all over me
I was so traumatized, I could hardly speak

Inside the hospital's emergency room
I was only treated for my outer wounds
Family and friends who love me very much
Felt this horrid crime shouldn't be kept hush

There was much controvert surrounding the case
Largely in part due to my black face
In months that followed my word bloomed full doubt
Judge ruled fabrication and threw the case right out

Rape is devastating whether it happen to a black or white
I know cause I lived it four days and three nights
I thank God for my life and for seeing me through
He'll see guilty parties get justice due

RAPE LADY

I was kidnapped one night
while walking the street
By two teen aged boys
and a rough young lady

Forced to perform on each
an oral sex act
She viciously rammed my vagina
with a wired coat rack

When they finally stopped
torturing me
She's the one who kicked me
back out on the street

I gave police their license number
that I'd written down
Her mom thought she could do no wrong
and hid her out of town

Just because I choose
to hook for a living
Does not mean
that I am without feeling

POWERLESS

At five I was molested by the school bus driver
When I finally told my parents they managed to have him fired
In all outward appearances I appeared to be fine
All the hurt was buried in that little heart of mine

Three years ago at the age of thirty-three
I found myself suffering irrationally
When my pre-school children defied my order
I spanked them so hard it was along the beating border

Parents Anonymous helped me out with my behavior
From there I went to therapy which helped even greater
Talking to the therapist made me realize
There was still much anger buried down inside

I now know that my rage stemmed from earlier experiences
Back to when I was young and powerless
Parents take care of your children after abuse is discovered
The healing need to begin at once so they can recover

ADOPTIVE RAPIST

Me and my twin were adopted and raped for eleven years
Sexual abuse occurred daily by the University of California teacher
Forced to have sex with him, male students, and other children
There were many pictures taken of the sick perversion

When developing his pictures in the university's lab
He'd become so aroused right there he'd make us gap
He told both my sister and I "do not tell"
"If you do your twin will end up going to jail"

On one weekend trip we took up to his cabin
He took five girls and made us all sleep nude with him
When his wife found out she thought of his reputation
She kept quiet, we fell in a spiral of self-destruction

Abused three more years we felt it was time
With a lawyer's help we're suing for every dime
More important though is to make everyone aware
This can happen to anyone, anytime, anywhere

SCARRED

Both me and my brother
were put up for sale
By our cocaine addict mother
who informed us "not to tell"

Most of the johns
were great-grandpa types
Little kids are who they
seemed to best like

She traded us
for some stupid dope
Mentally it scarred us
and left us without hope

BURST OPEN

At six months old mom held my legs
so daddy could come inside
He burst me wide open
I laid there and died

I'll never understand why
they were so cruel to me
I'll never understand why
they couldn't just let me be

I am much happier
up here with my Lord
Looking down I see
the problem have gotten worst

TAMPERED

Rushed to the hospital
when I was two weeks old
My brother crammed his
finger into my hole

When mom changed me
blood was in my pamper
That's when she discovered
my vagina had been tampered

I hope in the future
she keep a closer watch
Against his strength
I'm no kind of match

DAD'S SEX MATE

*I ran away from my
neat little home
Because my daddy
wouldn't leave me alone*

*I tried telling mom
what was going on
She thought with me
something was wrong*

*So out the door
I headed straight
I didn't like being
my dad's sex mate*

FILTHY RAPIST

We lived in a dark filthy apartment
As virtual prisoners with our parents
Raped, sodomized and beaten in our gloomy room
We weren't allowed outside not even for school

For us this was the only way of life
We may have had other siblings who didn't survive
Neighbors who cared called the authorities
All nine of us were taken immediately

Three months later they arrested mom and dad
For treating us all so very bad
We thank God for coming to our rescue
And are looking forward to starting life anew

ILL INCEST

Psychiatric counseling I'm now undergoing
My own daddy inside me went hoeing
When mother learned of the ill incest
She told his army peers who in turn made an arrest

Out the window went all his pension money
For they didn't like sleeping business funny
He was discharged ————dishonorably
Man who'd sleep with daughter is nothing but a S-L-E-A-Z-E!

He received fifteen years behind bars
Surely this will teach keep hands from me far
I am really glad I got it off my chest
Now at night when sleep I sincerely rest

SICK MOLEST

On the front room couch
my cousin felt all over me
Said if I ever told
he'd kill my family

"Don't move left or right!"
he threatened
And kept on
maliciously petting

It wasn't until a decade later
when I relieved my chest
That's when I, no longer afraid
told of the sick molest

CHILD CARE RAPISTS

Today I was molested
at my child care facility
By the people who were
taking care of me

After mom picked me up
I was very quiet
Later on that night
I couldn't hold in the vomit

Afterwards I told
that I had been hurt
By a bad man doctor
and a bad lady nurse

ON CHILD CARE CENTERS

In some of our nation's child care centers
Is where some of our kids genitals are first entered
So unless you feel you really can trust
At home with them stay — that is a must

GREAT SORROW

Unfortunately some victims do not survive
Because they're beaten and raped so badly they die
As was the case of a young beautiful girl
Who was loved by all who knew her in this world

Walking home one day from the ice cream shop
In the church house she decided a brief stop
A Sunday school teacher's sex advances she rejected
A heartless rape, murder she unfortunately was subjected

Her loved ones noticed her missing right away
Pinned her pictured posters all over the North Bay
When in some garbage bags her precious body was found
There was great sorrow all throughout town

How could something so awful happen to one so neat?
She was so young and innocent with a smile so sweet
We know she's at rest up there in the sky
Happy with our Lord sweet by and by

NEIGHBORLY RAPIST

Me and my brother were invited to clubhouse
By a neighbor friend who turned out to be a louse
He quickly locked the door once we were inside
We had no idea he had sex on his mind

He threatened us both not to make a sound
And before we knew it his pants and shorts were down
Helpless I watched in pain as he hurt my little brother
Forcefully he humped me too said "do not tell your mother!"

We were sore from having been forced in our rear end
We never told and never went there again
Somehow we knew what he did wasn't right
But were much too young to put up a fight

PORNOGRAPHY

Mom's boyfriend only interest was getting to me
To present me to the world of pornography
He asked if I'd like to make some easy money
Said there would be nothing to it at all funny

Seemed easy twenty dollars just to dance
But when I got there he forced off my pants
Most humiliating were the movie cameras going
Capturing dirty sex to me he was doing

I was so afraid to tell mother what he'd done
So I packed up my things and ran away from home
I told father I just had to get away
I never told either of them that I had been raped

EXECUTIVE RAPIST

I met a bank executive through
Big Brothers organization
Soon after we were friends
he engaged me in sexual relations

At his Lake Tahoe home
he was obsessed with me
I was continuously assaulted and
subjected to lewdness pornography

"Sorry,very sorry" he told
the judge for what he'd done
Seven years elapsed that
I endured this wrong

Some said the conviction destroyed
his twenty-five year banking career
I feel that I'm the one
who was destroyed here

MOLESTED

Looking through the window I saw
my oldest sister and brother
Naked in bed
having sex with each other

I was very shocked
couldn't believe my eyes
When she molested me
I felt so bad inside

My hatred for women
lasted very long
I knew what she
had did to me was wrong

Grown up I asked her
why had she bothered me
She said that our father had
abused her sexually

REBOUND MOLESTER

I am a victim
of molestation
I'm also guilty
of the same violation

I did some awful things
underneath the covers
To each one
of my younger brothers

I hope one day they can
forgive their big sis
Maybe if I'd gotten help
it wouldn't have come to this

PROM RAPE

The first time I had sex
I was brutally raped
By the guy who took me
on my senior prom date

He felt as though
I owed him my body
Said he was nice enough
to have taken me

Despite he'd given me bruises
broken ribs and two black eyes
I was called "strange, stupid"
for not giving in to the guy

Not once was I
viewed as the victim
After all they said
it's not like I didn't know him

I'm afraid of sex and
have opted for celibacy
Sometimes get the impression
that something is wrong with me

TORMENTED

Raped, robbed and beaten I felt
compelled to leave my home
My dog was nearly killed
I can't stand to be alone

I'm so scared and tormented
don't know what to do
At times I feel like running, running
the problem is where to?

No matter what my future
life will never be the same
Already without vision
now I feel completely lame

SEX FIENDS

One night we went joy riding
with two neighbor guys
When suddenly they stopped
and wanted to come inside

We were so scared
didn't know what to do
Somehow we got away
were two damnest running fools

In that old blue truck
they searched left and right
We hid behind a bush
well out of their sight

Tired of looking
they finally went on
We were relieved and walked
all the way back home

Can't trust anyone
this just goes to show
Not when they are
fiending down below

ILL RAPE

At a campus party
he said he was ill
Politely I helped him to his dorm
where he suddenly healed

Before I realized it
he was raping me
I was so shocked
I couldn't even scream

RAPE DAD

Mom knew dad was having
sex with me all along
More important to her was that
he brought the paycheck home

When I asked her if
she would make him stop
She accused me of
having seduced my pop

RAPED OR MOLESTED?

*If you've been raped or molested
you must get some help
Do not for one minute
blame it on yourself*

*Regardless how hard it may
seem to you at first
It's better to "let it out"
before the pain get worst*

*If you try to cover it
later on down the road
Life will be conflicting
heavier will be the load*

*If you care
for sanity
one thing you must do*

*Get some counsel
deal with it now
I promise you will get though*

MUST TELL

If you've been raped
you must tell someone
So you can get the help
that you need to move on

Don't think it'll go away
and just let you be
You really have to deal with it
in order to be free

NO LONGER FREE

At an early age
my virtue was forced from me
I no longer felt like a child
I no longer felt free

He said "do not worry
it happens everyday"
And that sooner or later
it was bound to come my way

For years I tried
not to think about it
But it kept coming up
no matter how hard I fought it

When finally able to talk out
the anger, hurt and pain
I stopped feeling
so terribly ashamed

Now I'm at peace
and happy once again
I know now I wasn't responsible
for his awful sin

MUST TALK

Though it may have happened
a long long time ago
It may just be why
your spirits are down low

With someone you must
talk out all the hurt
Only then will you be free
and able to move forth

HURT

*As a young girl
when I was raped
I felt lots of hurt*

*As a young girl
when I was raped
I felt just like dirt*

*As a young girl
when I was raped
I felt icky inside*

*As a young girl
when I was raped
I just wanted to die*

VIOLATED

*I once knew nothing about sex
that is until one day
My person was violated upon
in an ill-mannered way*

*I felt really low
dirty and disgusted
Culprit was someone I knew
and once had even trusted*

*My virtue he just took away
he said "it was no big deal"
He didn't give a dam
how bad it made me feel*

*He finished up
then just went
about his merry way*

*But for me
it was the beginning
of many a hellish day*

NO RIGHT!

Cause it's brother, dad or any other kin
Gives them no right to commit the sin
Of violating and taking away from you
Your virtue which in my point of view

Is yours to part with when you're d-a-m ready
No one has the right to force you to bed
So do yourself a favor if it happens to you
Tell all the world and his mamma too!

NEVER TOLD

After being raped
for a second time
I never told and tried to
put it out of my mind

I couldn't bear twice
going through the system
Of the courts who seemed to
care less about the victim

Over the years my heart
was filled with so much hate
I never realized it
stemmed back to the rapes

The more I talked about it
the better I began to feel
Getting it out is what I needed
for my heart to heal

MISERY

I had a baby
by my own father
It's still hard to accept
him raping his own daughter

I left the child in
the hospital's nursery
I couldn't bear being
reminded of the misery

In spite of what he did
mom stayed with him
I don't know if I'll ever
forgive either of them

CAN'T TELL

I have a mouth that can't tell anyone
when he molest me just for fun
I have feet but cannot run away
when he fondles me
and think it is o.k.

I have fingernails that
can't scratch his eyes
when his oversized p-thing
tears open my insides

Who am I?

A newborn
unable
to protect myself from harm

I may be old as two or three
still without strength
to fight my way free

At the age of
four, five or six
unable to
beat him with a stick

Seven, eight, nine or ten
frightened to silence
raped over again

Eleven or twelve
ashamed
walking with a down head
wishing I was dead

ASSAULTED

At the age of six I was
raped by my step dad
For many years I thought
I had done something bad

He'd told me that if I
ever told anyone
The police would come
and take him from our home

Also mom would lose her job
and it would be all my fault
That's why I never told
anyone about the assault

MY FAULT?

I was a young victim
of sexual assault
But was made to feel
as if it were my fault

Police locked me in a room
for a real long time
When they finally appeared
suggested I was lying

I was shocked because
I knew nothing of sex
So how in hell could I've
concocted such a hoax?

It was worst in court
he pleaded "not guilty"
His lawyer did all he could
to make me look filthy

Judge opened up the door
and told him to go home
I'd never felt so betrayed
or so all alone

I tried hard to forget
the hurting and the pain
But after many years have found
deep in it has remained

SILENT TEARS

I was so happy
until that day
he took something
so precious away

Softly I've cried
through the years
Holding back
pain and tears

Emotions fluctuate
up and down
One minute a smile
the next a frown

I have tried to
keep it out mind
But seem it's ever
so deeply ingrained

BETRAYED

*When children are
sexually abused
They feel betrayed and
their minds are confused*

*The best way to help them
through such an ordeal
Is to get them help so
their little hearts can heal*

*Ask God to
give them peace within
Instill they weren't responsible
for the rotten sin*

SEX ABUSE

Unfortunately sex abuse
happens everyday
to people all over the world

The sad thing is
it's kept to a hush
most time when it occurs

MUST LISTEN

We must listen when
children drop us hints
Something by it is
bound to be meant

Their heavy hearts are tangled
in shock and disbelief
From us they seek comfort
understanding and relief

CONFUSED

Though I'm away from home
I do not feel free
I've never told mom
what daddy did to me

Should I tell or
should I let it go?
I am so confused
don't know what to do

TELL!

As a young girl I was
forewarned by my dear mother
To come to her and tell
if ever I was bothered

Home from kindergarten
about to take a nap
My uncle sat in a chair
exposed with his legs a gap

He asked if he could put
that awful thing in me
As loud as I could
I started to scream

Startled, he turned his head
I ran like a bat out of hell
Stayed out until my sister came
and first thing I did was tell

Dad told him "be glad you didn't
finish up what you started"
"Right now you'd be dead"
with that he quickly parted

After that
we never saw him again
It's too bad you can't
even trust your kin

MUCH BETTER!

*I feel so much better
now that it's all out
Gone is all that pain
and all of that self-doubt*

*If you too
are a silent victim
Please get help
now is the time*

SUFFERING

To innocent young children
it really is not fair
To cause them pain and suffering
their hearts just cannot bear

Before you think a thought
of hurting a little one
Think of all the sorrow
to them that will be done

LOW DOWN

Such a low down dirty
rotten selfish deed
To force yourself upon one
to fulfill your need

Why bother one so young
or to you not willing?
When there are many others
who can tend your feeling

It's really not worth the long
suffering caused by your action
For a few lousy seconds
of animal sextisfaction

SCUM!

*No good
lowdown
dirty
rotten
scummy
incestuous
cock robbing
sodomizing
BASTARD!
you have
no right
to force
your
slimy
icky
stanky
maggoty self
into a place
you know
you
are not
wanted
... bastard you!*

PRIVATE PARTS

Children with their smiles so bright
Please don't turn their day to night
By hurting their little private parts
Saddening their precious little hearts

AFTERWARDS

*Afterwards I didn't want
anything to do with men
I even found it hard
to talk to any of them*

*Emotions started surfacing
about one month later
Talking out the pain
has made me feel much better*

*It was very helpful
knowing I wasn't alone
Other victims put it behind
find happiness and move on*

ATTACKED

My first night at school
I was attacked
I froze and as best
I could relaxed

Off guard I kicked and
hurt him down below
Free I ran
as fast as I could go

Though he didn't get
to finish up the job
I still felt betrayed
my virtue was nearly robbed

Not until the next morning
did it really hit
That's when I raged
into a mad fit

My religious beliefs is
what has helped me through
Without dear Lord Jesus
don't know what I'd do

TERRIFIED

Terrified to tell anyone
what was happening to me
Scared to disobey him
after all he was my daddy

As I grew into my teens
it started getting worst
But I understood things better
than I did at first

Nevertheless I felt
dirty, worthless and cheap
Hatred for men inside me
was implanted very deep

I have always felt
that it was my fault
Worst than the actual
molesting is the guilt

ASHAMED

I didn't know having sex
with my dad was wrong
Every since I was a child
it has been going on

I felt no control over
my body or emotions
He bought me special gifts
and paid me lots of attention

When I learned it wasn't right
I tried getting him to stop
He didn't agree
and said that he would not

I was ashamed to have
strangers know my secret
But my friend convinced me
it was for the best

DESTROYED

At ten years old
I attempted suicide
Due to an incestuous childhood
that began when I was five

It took ten long years
and lots of help from my mate
To come to terms with it
and freely talk out the hate

My older sister thinks sex is
the dirtiest thing in the world
My younger sister don't care and is
a hooker as a young girl

Our father was wrong
for having hurt us all
We were destroyed while he was
having himself a ball

NASTY THINGS

Sexually aggressive
at seven years old
What I learned at home
has made me this bold

With other kids, when I
try letting off the steam
They think I'm weird
for doing nasty things

ROTTEN ORDEAL

Cause we can't use big words
to describe what was did
No one wants to believe us
innocent young kids

On the witness stand
lawyers make us feel
As if we're responsible
for the rotten ordeal

We don't know why
everyone rather blame us
We're to young to know about
any of this disgust

WRONGED

My uncle used to give me a quarter
to sit upon his lap
All the while he'd run his hand
right between my gap

At the time
I didn't know it was wrong
Mom said she'd have killed him
if only she had known

I have told
my precious daughter
To tell if anyone touches her
that includes her father

EMBARRASSED

I started using drugs
soon after I was raped
I was so embarrassed
and thought I was gay

When my coach asked if I'd
like to go for a ride
I had no idea he would
tear open my behind

When he dropped me off
he said "do not tell"
Every since that day
I have not been well

DAMAGED

Raped by my big brother when I was just a kid
He have no idea the internal damage it has did
I never told mom, dad wasn't alive to tell
It's been twenty years that I've lived with this hell

I didn't want anyone to know that this happened to me
Having another male inside made me feel like a freak
When I start unloading to a counselor
The heavy burden was lifted from my shoulder

As a man I feel much better about myself
I am glad that I finally sought help
If as a boy you too were sodomized
Get help today you'll feel much better inside

NIGHTMARE

I'm forty-two and still recovering from a nightmare
Raped from seven to twelve by my dad who didn't care
The sexual abuse caused me severe health problems
Also trouble in school, employment and social relations

I felt crazy but couldn't figure out why
Strange as it seems the connection wasn't realized
Survivors often have no memory of the crime
I spent twenty-five years blocking it out of my mind

With help from a psychologist, support groups and a loving husband
I'm beginning to feel like a normal person once again
Incestuous families have a "no talk" rule that keep the incest going
It's imperative the awful secret be brought out into the opening

INTOLERABLE

As a grown up I kept
having recurring nightmares
Couldn't put my finger on it but
I always woke up scared

It took three long years of
extensive therapy
Before I remembered as a child
being abused sexually

The violence was so intolerable
I'd totally blanked it out
It was responsible for
a lot of my self-doubt

Now that it's all out
into the opening
I function much better
as a human being

PAINFUL

*Mom's boyfriend raped me
when I was eight years old
He threatened to kill my brother
if I ever told*

*I must have slipped unconscious
while he was raping me
When I awoke he was
washing off my body*

*I put on my clothes
and hurried outside
There was painful burning
between my small thighs*

*I stayed in bed
after returning home
I felt really bad
and wanted to be alone*

*When mom found
blood stains in my panties
I was still afraid to tell
who'd did that to me*

*When my brother convinced me
that he would not die
I went ahead and told
as we both sat there and cry*

SKI MASK RAPIST

I am a tiny fragile
eighty-four year old
Raped at gunpoint in
the Church Confessional

Asked to pull up my blouse
told to do a sex act
He put a gun to my head
when I said I can't

"I've killed other people
and will kill you too"
That's what he said to me
before the abuse

When he was caught I couldn't
positively identify
He raped many women
in a ski mask disguise

His wife was also
indicted along with him
For receiving property
he stole from his victims

STRIP SEARCH RAPISTS

I was paid fifty thousand dollars
in an out of court settlement
After I was raped by
three deputy sheriff men

Stopped for a drunk driving
test in which I fail
I was arrested, beaten
fondled and thrown in jail

Stripped, searched and raped
later on that night
By all three who supposedly
work for what is right

PAINFULLY ENTERED

Raped by my counselor
when I was very young
I was too afraid to tell
anyone what he'd done

Out of all the boys
I was his pick
Every time he touched me
inside I felt sick

I was all confused about
my sexuality
Feelings of being a homosexual
I repeatedly washed my body

One day he pretended
we were going to dinner
He drove to his house instead
from behind I was painfully entered

Thirty-five years passed
before I told my dad
The rotten things he did to me
when I was a lad

SLEAZE

I was raped but
never told anyone
I packed some of my things
and ran away from home

I thought if I left
dad would be o.k.
A few months later
my little sister ran away

Living on the streets
haven't been very easy
But it's better then living with
a dad who is sleazy

AX RAPIST

Raped and left with two chopped off arms
By a man who I accepted a ride from
He stopped to release himself on the road
Hit me across my back as I squat to unload

He tied up my hands and raped me in his van
Made me drink liquor raped me over, over again
I was very weak, from the alcohol I passed out
When I finally came to he ordered me to"get out!"

"You want to be free?" he asked
Chopped off both arms with an ax
Shoved down an embank stuffed in concrete pipe
I walked three miles in tears I could not wipe

Next morning I was found dressed only in my skin
Holding arms and muscles trying to keep blood in
Prospective hitchhikes please be forewarned
You might suffer sexual and physical harm

SUBURB RAPE

Raped and sodomized by
affluent sports stars
Despite my condition of
being a mildly retard

Lured from the park
to their cushy suburb
Eight of them looked on
as I was raped by others

I was raped with harsh objects
and forced to perform sex acts
Among objects were a broomstick
and miniature baseball bat

When I told my teachers
what they did to me
Police weren't notified
for another three weeks

One of the onlookers was
a police lieutenant's son
When asked about the case
replied "she wanted it done"

Their were five arrests including
brothers who co-captained the team
How could they be so callous to me
retarded and seventeen?

CAMPUS RAPE

As I brought in my
groceries from the store
He emerged as I was
about to shut the door

Smiling he flashed
a large pocket knife
Right before my eyes
went my precious life

I told him to take anything
he yelled "shut up bitch!"
He kicked my belly and the
left side of my face was nitched

He took off his pants
forced me to my knees
"Do it now!"
he screamed at me

He seemed to enjoy
the terror in my eyes
Made me put on his condom
and rammed my insides

Looked at me and laughed
when he was finally through
From campus the next day
me and my roommate moved

CALLOUS ABUSER

Whenever mom refused
daddy in her bed
He slept with me
and my sister instead

Fondled, raped and sodomized
for fourteen long years
He callously abused us
despite our tears

He'd threaten to rape our youngest sister
if we didn't comply
We continued giving in
so she wouldn't have to cry

He moved out when I reported
to a counselor at school
We're suing him for compensation
for years of being treated so cruel

PASTOR RAPE

I was sexually abused
in a Florida hotel
By a man who preach
about heaven and hell

He invited me to a
P.T.L. telethon
Once we were there
I was forced upon

I had planned on staying
a virgin for my husband
To keep it quiet he paid me
two hundred sixty-five grand

I hid the story for
seven l-o-n-g years
Came close to suicide
there were many tears

To a different pastor
and businessman I confided
Literally tore apart
I could no longer hide it

HELL THREAT RAPE

"You might go to hell if
you don't have sex with me"
That's what the minister told
members of our church assembly

He raped and sodomized
me and my little sister
He's also guilty of raping
another parishioner

In all outward appearances
he was a model citizen
However, there existed a dark side
that betrayed and violated women

"A wolf in sheep's clothing"
is how some described him
He was sentenced twenty-one years
for his awful crime

BUSH RAPED

I was out for an
early morning run
Out of nowhere he
accosted me with a gun

Dragged behind a bush
by the rotten man
Who raped me over
and over again

Didn't want family told
after I called police
I preferred their minds
to remain at peace

I was totally calm
until the exam room
I went all to pieces when
the doctor touched my womb

Counselor from Rape Crisis Center
God bless her little heart
Was there to hold my hand and
help keep me from coming apart

It's too bad there's no
respect for elderly
You'd think with being old
that they'd let us be

DERANGED RAPIST

During a routine
dental examination
I was put under
heavy medication

Somewhat conscious but
unable to get up
I was raped for hours
by the deranged nut

After court he lost his license
and moved to a new state
I hear he's practicing again
both dentistry and rape

RAPE COP

Sitting in my car
chatting with a friend
An on duty police walked up
and ordered me to go with him

He drove to a nearby
auto body shop
Led me to a storage room
where he retrieved a cot

I was raped and forced
to oral copulate
His partner stood outside
by the door to wait

During the lawsuit
I was arrested unlawfully
Rape charges were dropped
after he pleaded guilty

He got off with two years
probation and a misdemeanor
Ordered to resign his post
and scolded for keeping me prisoner

BLIND RAPE

Not one single thing
can I see
He still had
no mercy on me

He held his hands
tight over mouth
Then raped me
before running out

I used my sense
of touch and smell
To identify the scum
who put me through hell

Now they don't know
if court can receive
My only form
of identity

"It's not enough to stand
in a court of law"
Always getting away with
some technical flaw

RETARDED RAPIST

I'm severely retarded
but that didn't stop him
From adding me to the
statistics of rape victims

Not only was I raped
in the care group home
He left behind
a baby in my womb

The case is too difficult
to go through litigation
Due to my
limited communication

HUMILIATED

Jogging the wooded path
at the university
Zipping up his pants
he jumped from behind a tree

I ran faster
trying to get away
He was determined and
also picked up pace

He drug me down a slope with
his hands over my mouth
Raped me on the ground
and warned me not to shout

Humiliation dominates
despite therapy
I'm still very shaken
it won't let me be

I decided to
go on and finish school
To this day I haven't told
my parents the awful news

BLOOD RAPE

*I'm confined to a
bed on wheels
He raped me
despite my being ill*

*He came into my room
as soon as everyone left
Took off my clothes and
forcefully helped himself*

*My blood brother did
this awful thing to me
Thanks I get for allowing
him to stay here free*

VAIN ABUSE

Home at state hospital
for the mentally ill
We were made to have
sex against our will

Given illicit drugs by
the psychiatric technician
To weaken us further
right before he dug in

He also used excess force
and unlawful restraints
When he molested and
abused us in vain

Boldly he raped at
four in the afternoon
Right inside the girl's
dormitory room

Already fragile to
physical and sex abuse
We came here for help
not for further use

KIDDIE PORN

A normal childhood
I missed out on
My parents made me star
in kiddie porn

I've always felt
dirty and low
Even when I wanted
I couldn't say no

A prostitute
is what I am today
Really, I don't know
any other way

DRUNK RAPIST

Beaten and raped by my drunk husband
over a period of time
Each time I called police they'd say
he's guilty of no crime

When I got a gun and shot
the shit out his ass
This time when they came
they made an arrest at last

Now crime has been committed
they locked me up and said
The only regret I have
is that he isn't dead

CONDO RAPE

National football player
who wouldn't accept no
Raped me inside of his
Atlantic condo

Forced to perform sex
I was also sodomized
With a wine bottle
he threatened my life

Once upon a time
we were mutual friends
Should've gotten a willing person
at his other end

ALCOHOLIC RAPIST

My alcoholic father began
raping me at five
When I found courage to tell
mom called me a troublemaker and a lie

For several weeks I cried, pleaded
threw up and had nightmares
Mom walked around as though
she didn't even care

Then one day she said
"I'll leave it up to you"
Added "police will take him to jail,
we'd starve and might die too"

Being an insecure, emotionally
and troubled ten year old
The sex abuse went on
I could not bear that load

About one year later
he finally left me alone
Began abusing two younger cousins
who lived in our home

CORRUPT

*I had a child
many years ago
After being raped by
a guy I used to know*

*I held it once
after it was born
Felt nothing but contempt
as I held it in my arm*

*I have no regrets
that I gave it up
I felt it would have
made my life corrupt*

OCCUPATIONAL RAPIST

Sick at home one day
when a bogus delivery man
Came to my door with
a package in his hand

When I opened the door
he threatened my life
Then raped me while
brandishing a knife

Beverly Hills policeman
was once his occupation
He watched me at the playground
before committing the violation

CHILD RAPIST

My uncle raped six kids
in our family
Our kin took him to court
where he was found guilty

With a smart lawyer
he appealed the verdict
He's walking free though
it's known he's pedophilic

With enough money you can get away
with anything these days
That includes a crime
as horrible as child rape

INCEST

Some days it was
more than three
When dad came home
to rape me

Though I tired
of the incest
Not one day
he gave me rest

The only thing
that made him stop
Is when I reported
him to the cop

UNBEARABLE

I paid a thousand dollars
To have my father killed
Because he started raping me
after mom took ill

He ordered me to watch t.v.
in him and mother's room
That is where he would
tear apart my womb

When I asked him
"why are you doing this?"
He replied
"there's nothing wrong with it"

He raped me more and more
after mom was dead
I couldn't bear to look at him
and covered up my head

When he started looking
at my baby sister
I couldn't bear
the thought of her in tears

PETTED

Each night after dinner
sitting on daddy's lap
He petted all over me while
my drunk mom pretended to nap

This happened from age
three until twelve
He didn't seem the least
ashamed of himself

When my friends told me this
didn't happen with their dad
That's when I realized
he was doing something bad

He became angry when
I started saying no
He also became
verbally abusive and cold

Grown up I sought help
for this past ill
My parents refused joint counseling
and cut me out of their will

UGLY RAPIST

I was fast asleep in my
safe security building
When suddenly I woke
to a bangy feeling

When he first struck
I thought I was dreaming
When he struck again
that's when I started screaming

He secured a blindfold
tight over my eyelids
Said the reason for it was
to keep his ugliness hid

I was repeatedly beaten
raped and sodomized
When he said he always killed
I stopped fighting and complied

He left with twenty dollars
I had to untie myself
I called up my parents
who rushed over to help

My neighbor above who'd heard said
she thought something wasn't right
But didn't want to get involved
and turned off her light

SHOCKED

My teacher showed a special interest in me
Took me home one day to show me something neat
She couldn't find it once we were there
And returned to the room naked as a bear

Frozen there I stood in a state of shock
I was hardly able to keep up my sock
She moved closer to assure all was o.k.
Next thing I knew we were rolling in the hay

Only thing she wanted to show me unique
Was her overgrown naked physique
The real reason I was her special boy
Was so she could use me for her sexual joy

MANSION RAPE

In the governor's executive mansion
our sixteen year old was raped
By four teen aged boys
while their parents were away

Though three unnamed were minors
everyone think they know
All involved in treating
our girl like a hoe

Eighteen year old pleaded guilty
to under age drinking
I can't see what anyone
of them scums were thinking

FONDLED

He followed me into the lobby
of my apartment building
Then inside the elevator
where he began fondling

When he got off
I went up another floor
Rushed in and told my dad
what had just occurred

Dad looked out the window
spotted him on the sidewalk
Chased him to the subway station
where he was then caught

Police think he's the exhibitionist
who stalked other children
I am glad that
they finally caught him

DISGUSTING RAPISTS

I was kidnapped at two years old
They raped my body, they raped my soul
By forcing their great big selves into me
With those things that they use to pee

They kept me cooped up in a dirty van
Did things to me I didn't understand
They had also kidnapped another
Who watched over me like a brother

One day we sneaked from that awful place
To the police we quickly raced
They went to arrest those disgusting creeps
Who for a long time made us weep

GANG RAPED

I was gang raped
by three young men
One of whom left
a baby within

Don't know which one
of them fathered her
Don't know what to tell
my beautiful daughter

NURSERY MOLESTER

On a Sunday morning
in the Church's nursery
Instead of baby sitting
he was molesting me

In treatment he was urged
to disclose the names
Of other kids who he'd
also did this shame

Sixty-three children aged
one and a half to four
This dreadful thing
also had occurred

How would he know how to
carry on this way at ten?
What are we teaching
our young gentlemen?

INFANTILE RAPES

Year after year I was
slept with by my father
Mom knew but it didn't
seem to bother her

I was an emotional crippled mute
from the infantile rapes
Remnants of that legacy
I never escaped

I've never been able
to trust in any man
Nor form a genuine friendship
with any woman

I am old now
and have suffered long
For terrifying me, dad
—and mom—were wrong

MANIAC

I just f....d your sister
rapist said to his girlfriend
She stayed with him
despite his dreadful sin

I did all
I could to forget
When they had a child
she asked me to baby sit

When he started looking
like that maniac
It kept reminding me
of the rape attack

Unconsciously
I was angry at him
Later realized it was
because of his father's crime

RAPED

Home alone one afternoon as I lay in my bed
My sister's naughty boyfriend came in and said
"I raped and killed a girl in Detroit, Michigan"
"Will do the same to you if you don't give in"

He asked "what position would you like to try?"
I'd never been with a man "none" I replied
He ripped off my clothes and tore into me
Over and over he screamed "spread apart your feet!"

He gave me a dollar said "go buy ice cream at the store"
Reminded me "do not tell" again, then raced out the door
With towel and hot water crying in the bathroom
I tried wiping all of his filth from my womb

My aunt came I told, she called police, he showed up again
She asked why, he looked through me as if I had sinned
In separate cars we were taken to the station
I was treated as if I committed the violation

When the chief finished interrogating me
My eyes were so teary I could hardly see
When it got to court the maniac kept saying
"I am innocent of the alleged laying"

My sister helped none she was on his side
"Judge he did not" on the witness stand she LIED
He was freed and I tried burying the hurt
I wanted to forget having been treated as dirt

ADMINISTRATIVE RAPIST

Former chief administrative officer
and ex-mayor candidate of San Francisco
Was caught raping teenagers in a
Mission district bordello

I knew I'd seen his picture
on a campaign billboard
But wasn't sure at first cause
he'd said his name was "George"

For seven counts of rape
he was found guilty
But on his sentencing
they went light and easy

They said he was embarrassed
by the situation enough
He was fined one-hundred thousand dollars
and told to sweep streets up

When important officials
are involved in sex crimes
They pay their way out
every single time

SHAMED

I was raped
after a baseball game
Didn't tell because
I was so ashamed

I delivered a son
nine months later
My love for him
couldn't be any greater

His dad I don't
think much of
Blessed am I
from the Man above

FORCED INTO

When my parents died I went to live
with my uncle and aunt
Whenever left alone with him
he forced into my pants

"Won't do any good to tell
no one will believe you"
That's what he'd tell me
each time he was through

I'm grateful to my aunt for
providing a home for me
But felt I had no choice
other than to leave

CAMPUS ABDUCTION

*On the way back
to my dormitory
I was abducted as I walked
from the campus library*

*Blindfolded, tied up
and driven to the woods
Where I was beaten
and raped by two hoods*

*After several hours
they finally let me go
I had to find my way back
from the deserted road*

*Mom thinks I'm wrong
for carrying a gun
I'll do what's necessary
for my protection*

NASTY SEX

After watching a nasty
sex scene on t.v.
My twelve year old stepbrother
tried it on me

First in the morning
then again that afternoon
When I went to use it
the pee stung my womb

My mom rushed me to
the hospital's emergency
There doctors told her
I'd been entered forcefully

He was charged with rape, incest
and lewd and lascivious acts
At five years old I was not
ready for life's facts

RAPE COUSIN

Left in my cousin's care
when I was nine years old
He raped me but
I never told

The next morning
he took me to the zoo
To keep me quiet
he bought me ice cream too

I knew it was wrong but, didn't
realize it wasn't my fault
Finger of blame would point to me
is what I thought

Later when I found out
how babies were made
I thought that I was
pregnant from the rape

Whenever my stomach hurt
I rushed to the bathroom
So nobody would see
the infant leave my womb

It didn't occur until years later
that I'd been sexually abused
I was quite surprised to learn
it happened to others too

PINSTRIPE RAPIST

I was raped by a man
clothed in his pinstripe best
While I sat in my car one morning
studying for a test

Shoved to the passenger's side
as he reclined the seat
He covered my face with my jacket
and screamed "don't look at me!"

Forced to oral copulate him
after he drove to another area
He attempted sodomy then
painfully tore in my vagina

Finished, he pulled his pants
and covered my face again
Before leaving he stole
my wedding ring and band

Collected, I drove to the hospital
screamed "I've just been raped!"
A nurse came quickly
and whisked me away

RETALIATORY RAPE

As I walked near Nevin
and Macdonald avenue
I was kidnapped and raped in retaliation
for something I didn't do

Pointing a gun
he ordered me to get in
He said he was almost killed
by one of my friends

Drove to an unknown locale
I was raped and tied up
He repeatedly stabbed my neck
and left me bleeding in the tub

After a couple of hours
he put a towel around my neck
Wrapped me in a shower curtain
and threw me in the trunk

He dumped me in a parking lot
near the Nimitiz freeway
There I was found by a police
around ten o'clock that day

AWFUL RAPIST

When I spent weekends over daddy's house
He fondled me under my pants and blouse
At his house we bathed together in the tub
Playing with himself he'd tell me to rub

One day he stuck his "man thing" inside
It hurt me so bad I sat there and cried
I told mommy he hurt me bad down there
And was doing things to me I couldn't bear

With daddy I really did not want to lay
Judge said I had to go with him anyway
Mom decided she would rather go to jail
And sent me away from that awful hell

I know it's hard to be away from her little girl
But she loves me more than anything in this world
Each night when I go to bed I pray
Lord may this nightmare be over for me someday?

SCARED

At two she graphically described
oral sex with her father
Judge granted "probable but not proved"
he was doing this to our daughter

She'd come home from her visits
hysterically crying and screaming
Her hymenal ring was enlarged
and there was fibrous scarring

He claim it was caused from
"bike riding and straddled chairs"
If that was really the case
why is she so scared?

PROMINENT MOLESTER

Prominent lawyer is now
the subject of litigation
For sexual battery
and child molestation

I was at the bus stop
waiting at two a.m.
When he drove up and asked me
to do sexual favors for him

After declining
I telephoned the cops
Who found another young man
with him down a few blocks

Young man told officers
he offered him a ride
And fondled him sexually
while he was inside

He was arrested
booked and thrown in jail
Unfortunately was released
after he posted bail

ROTTEN THINGS

My father used to
mean the world to me
Until he forced away
my virginity

Shortly afterwards
I left home
Couldn't bring myself
to even talk to mom

This all happened
over ten years ago
But I still find that
it bothers me so

How can any father
do this to his own son?
I can't seem to stop thinking
about rotten things he done

SENSELESS

Shame one can't jog safely in the park
Just because it's after dark
Beaten by a gang of thugs
Who raped and left me to die in my blood

For no apparent reason they attacked
Raped, beat and tossed me forth and back
When they finished there I lie
Miraculously I didn't die

My health will never be the same
This senseless crime has left me lame
Shame one can't jog safely in the park
Just because it's after dark

SEXUAL TRANSGRESSOR

When I remarried
I had no idea
My husband's only interest
was my daughter's vagina

I came home from work one day
and found him humping inside
My nine year old baby
telling her "do not cry"

Arrested and imprisoned
for his bold transgression
I pray to God she'll be o.k.
after therapy sessions

SEVERELY ABUSED

I was mentally and sexually abused
By my stepfather and mother beginning at age two
As a result I have ninety-two personalities
Each persona carry a different memory

One of us remember being hung down a well
Terrified when snakes came swarming down like hail
Another recall him trying to make us touch his thing as well as the cat's
When we refused to do either he became very mad

One day we saw him having sex with the cow
Though we ran fast, he caught us anyhow
We screamed he tore our pants and held us in front
Bare naked up to the cow's pink caterpillar tongue

Whenever the mother discovered stepfather's cruel sex games
If she couldn't get through to him, we suffered her vengeful pain
On occasion when he wanted a change of pace
He'd sit us on the table and ejaculate in our face

He started on me again the night I came from my prom
The mother stepped in with a gun, told him to leave our home
After fourteen years the damage had already settled in
Soon after we left home and have survived as best we can

Tired of hiding, we take three baths a day
We still feel dirty, it doesn't go away
When we began therapy we insisted he videotape
Each of the sessions to help others who've been raped

VICTIM'S PRAYER

If I am a victim of sexual assault
Help make me realize it wasn't my fault

If I am a victim of molestation
Heal me of mental devastation

If I am a victim of incest
Help my family realize non-kin is best

If I am a victim who's just a kid
Help me to best describe what was did

If I have turned in the blame
Help me to stop feeling ashame

If I am stagnant from the hurt
Help me to utilize all my self-worth

If I was transmitted a sexual disease
Curable one I pray, so mind can ease

If I haven't told any yet
Help me to get it off my chest

Father these things I ask each day
In Jesus Christ your Son I pray

       Amen

SEXUAL

ABUSE

INFORMATION

MYTHS AND FACTS ABOUT RAPE

"Rapists are strange men in dark alleys."
> Fact: Over 1/3 of the rape victims are "friends" of the rapist. About 1/3 of the assaults occur in the victim's home.

"Rape is the result of uncontrollable passion."
> Fact: Most victims and place where the rape occur are premeditated.

"Women ask for rape by dressing provocatively."
> Fact: Rapists plan their targets and are not looking for women dressed in any particular way.

"Women want to be raped."
> Fact: Women do not enjoy being the victim of this violent and humiliating crime.

"Only young women are raped."
> Fact: Victims range in age from two months to ninety-two years. Males—children, teenagers and sometimes, men—are also victims.

"You can spot a rapist anywhere."
> Fact: Sex offenders are "normal looking" people from all walks of life.

FACTS ABOUT RAPE

Rape is a violent sexual crime which causes fear, injury, humiliation and psychological trauma. It is a crime of violence, not passion. Sexual assault is used to express anger, power, control and dominance.

All women are potential rape victims regardless of age, race, class, religion, occupation or physical description. Sometimes even males are the victims of rape.

Rape can occur anywhere at anytime, in public or in your home, day or night. A rapist will rape again and again, generally, in the same area and in the same manner.

Rapists are not necessarily strangers. In fact, in over 1/3 of reported cases, the rapist is an acquaintance, neighbor, friend or relative of the victim.

Most rapists appear to be normal. They come in all races, color and economic backgrounds.

Most rapist carry a weapon or threaten the victim with violence or death. Forcible rape is increasing in this country more than any other violent crime.

Rape is one of the most under-reported crimes. The majority of rapists continue until caught. Report any kind of sexual assault!

IF YOU ARE RAPED

Go to a safe place immediately.

Do not shower, bathe, wash your hands, brush your teeth or use toilet (you may destroy important evidence needed in court).

Do not clean up in anyway until you've talked to the police.

Call the police as soon as you can. The sooner you make the report the greater the chances the attacker will be caught.

Get medical attention as soon as possible.

Contact a friend or family member you can trust, call the Rape Crisis Center for support and information.

Remember, you are the victim. You have nothing to feel guilty or ashamed about. You may want to contact a treatment or crisis center to help you deal with the consequences of the assault.

HELP FOR VICTIMS

Rape Crisis Centers

Rape crisis centers provide direct assistance to victims of sexual assault. Such as:

1. Crisis intervention
2. In-person counseling
3. Follow-up counseling
4. Accompaniment to hospitals, criminal justice agencies and social service agencies
5. Information and referral
6. Community and school prevention programs
7. Self-defense programs
8. Training for law enforcement, medical, mental health and social service professionals.

If you have trouble locating a Rape Crisis Center in your local phone book, please call the

NATIONAL ABUSE HOT LINE at

1 800 422-4453

* These centers provide 24-hour support and all services are confidential and free.*

CHILD SEXUAL ASSAULT

Facts About Child Sexual Assault

Sexual abuse of children within the family is the most hidden, least publicized form of child abuse. In spite of its taboo nature and the difficulty of detection, some researchers believe such abuse may be even more common than physical abuse.

In discussing sexual abuse, "incest" means sexual activity between persons who are blood-related; "intrafamilial" refers to sexual activity between family members not related by blood (step-parents, boyfriends, etc.).

A person with no prior history of sexual problems can be tempted to sexually abuse a child in the intimacy of family life, especially at times of stress or when adult relationships are poor. A person who chooses to involve a child in sexual activity can easily make the child believe that sex is a special game or a normal and necessary part of being loved and accepted. An older child can be convinced that he/she is at fault for seducing the parent/caretaker. The child then fears disgrace, hatred or blame for breaking up the family if the secret is revealed.

CHILD SEXUAL ASSAULT

Facts About Child Sexual Assault

Although some adults may believe their conduct is blameless, the harm done to the child remains the same whenever sexual abuse is committed. The abuser may convince himself that he has a duty to "show the child the facts of life". He may believe he is more loving and caring than outsiders who might "spoil" or mistreat the child. He may feel so neglected and needy himself that he feels compelled to exploit the only loving relationship he can find. He may enter the child's bedroom at night and take down bed covers to expose the child's body or to explore it with hands or mouth. Confused and fearful of this strange, recurring behavior, the child usually pretends sleep. Sometimes, the abuser's approach is more direct. The child is courted and seduced into mutual arousal or forced to masturbate or fellatio the abuser. Vaginal intercourse also occurs even with quite young children, as well as with older children.

Sexual abuse is followed by guilt-provoking demands for se-crecy and/or threats of terrible harm if the secret is revealed. Regardless of how gentle or forceful or how trivial or coincidental the first experience may have been, sexual coercion tends to be repeated and escalated over a period of years. Often the child eventually accepts the blame for tempting and provoking the abuser.

CHILD SEXUAL ASSAULT

Facts About Child Sexual Assault

In most reported cases of sexual abuse, the father or another man acting as the parent is the initiator. While girls are the most frequent victims, boys are victims of abuse much more often than previously believed. The embarrassment and shame used to deter girls from reporting such abuse has an even greater effect on boys since the abuse is most often homosexual.

The initial sexual abuse may occur at any age, from infancy through adolescence. However, the largest number of cases involve females under the age of 11 years. The sexual activity is usually repetitive and progressive. There is no escape for the victim until he/she is old enough to realize that sexual abuse is not a common occurrence. And he/she is strong enough to obtain help outside the family.

The mother, who normally would be expected to protect the child may purposely try to stay isolated from a problem of sexual abuse. Sometimes she is distant and uncommunicative, or so disapproving of sexual matters that children are afraid to speak up. Sometimes, she is so insecure at the potential loss of her husband or partner and the fear of scandal is so threatening that she cannot allow herself to believe or even to suspect that her child is or could be at risk. She may have been victim herself of child abuse and rejection and may not trust her judgment or her right to challenge the male authority. Some mothers actually know of sexual abuse; but, for whatever reason, they look the other way.

CHILD SEXUAL ASSAULT

Facts About Child Sexual Assault

Sometimes a child who does seek help is accused of making up stories, since many people cannot believe that the apparently well-adjusted person involved could be capable of sexual abuse. When the matter does come to the attention of authorities, the child may give in to pressure from parents/caretakers and deny that any sexual abuse has occurred. Even if public attention is gained, the child may feel guilty about "turning in" the abuser or breaking up the family and, consequently, withdraw the complaint. This process leads many to be skeptical of the child's complaint of sexual abuse and leaves him/her feeling helpless and guilty for causing so much trouble. Everything in the secrecy and circumstances surrounding illicit sexual activity combines to make the victim carry the weight of the problem.

The sad reality is that the child often remains trapped in secrecy by shame, fear, and the threats of the abuser.

Careful evaluation is necessary in a sexual abuse situation to determine whether the child should be removed from the home immediately. The mother may assure the police or child protective services that the offending male will not be allowed to return to the home. However, in view of the emotional and, perhaps economic dependence the mother often has on the offending male, she may allow him back into the house. Thus, the child is again in an unprotected environment.

CHILD SEXUAL ASSAULT

Facts About Child Sexual Assault

Even though sexual abuse is often deceptively nonviolent, it is more powerfully compelling and more often disabling than any strong-arm attack from a stranger. Yet, the prognosis often can be encouraging. There can be a striking recovery when effective intervention and help are provided. Intervention alone does not interrupt the trap of sexual abuse, for the child remains burdened with guilt and helplessness unless the offending person is forced to admit and take responsibility for his/her actions. Detection, reporting, investigation, appropriate prosecution, supervision, and counseling are frequently essential parts of a family treatment process.

It is of the utmost importance to let your child know that he/she is not to blame for the assault. Try and get him/her to talk about it gently and without pressure.. If they don't wish to talk about it immediately, don't push. Reassure him/her that when he/she is ready, you'll be there to listen. It is important that your child talk out the hurt that he/she is feeling. Feelings bottled in too long reinforce self-blame which sometimes leads to self-destruction.

HELP FOR CHILDREN

Self-help organizations such as Children United, Parents United, and Parents Anonymous can be very helpful. They provide support and promote self-esteem and emotional well-being during the process of discovery, social intervention, adjudication, resocialization, and rebuilding of the family.

Early identification of abused children and clinical intervention is essential to develop healthy individuals and to prevent patterns from crossing generations.

For the organization nearest you please contact:

> *Parents United*
> *P. O. Box 952*
> *San Jose, CA 95108-0952*

SEXUAL ABUSE SHOULD BE SUSPECTED IF:

The child reports sexual activities with parents, other relatives, friends of the family, or other adults;

The child shows an early stage and exaggerated awareness of sex, with either seductive interest or fearful avoidance of close contacts with others;

There is tearing, bruising, or specific inflammation of the mouth, anus, or genitals, or evidence of semen (oral, rectal, vaginal);

There is venereal disease of the eyes, mouth, anus, or genitals of a child or adolescent;

A girl is pregnant and appears extremely fearful, distressed, or secretive;

A child with behavioral problems hints at conflicts at home, but seems quite hesitant or fearful to talk about the problem; and, or

A child is known to be the victim of other forms of abuse.

Remember, a victim of incest (intrafamillial) or child sexual abuse may, out of their pain, confusion, or anger, act out in any number of anti-social patterns. Some of which include becoming increasingly passive, attempting suicide, running away from home, becoming involved in drug and/or alcohol abuse, or committing criminal acts.

CHILD SEXUAL ASSAULTERS

Facts About Child Sexual Abusers

The term "child molester" usually refers to a male or female (but, most often, an older heterosexual male) who receives sexual gratification from young girls. A male (adult homosexual) or female who receives sexual gratification from young boys is commonly referred to as a "chicken hawk." The child molesters and chicken hawks usually have a specific age preference.

Chicken hawks and child molesters are "benevolent keepers" of their child victims. Many suspects are, in fact, wealthy and financially secure men or women who can afford to provide elaborate gifts for their victims. For most of their time together, the suspect caters to the child's wants and needs in an exaggerated, caring relationship. In return, the child willingly submits to sexual activity. While this perverse form of attention and affection may be especially appealing to an isolated runaway child, the danger of such sexual exploitation is certainly not limited to runaways. It can and does represent a danger to any child whose parent/caretaker fails to provide necessary attention and affection.

Pornographic literature is a device by which a suspect can steer a normal conversation with a juvenile towards a sexual theme. It is used to stimulate both suspect and victim and to assist in breaking down inhibitions. The nature of the literature usually will correspond with the suspect's particular sexual inclination, and the models used are usually of the age the suspect prefers.

CHILD SEXUAL ASSAULTERS

Facts About Child Sexual Abusers

The child abuser is typically a recidivist; that is, the abuser tends to repeat the abuse. The abuser is also typically an escalator in that the amount and severity of the abuse tends to increase. Because of these characteristics, early identification, reporting, and intervention are essential and vital.

Although many people assume that parents are the only culprits, it is important to remember that children can become victims of abuse by persons in non-parental relationships, such as foster parents, baby-sitters, day-care workers, etc.

Half of all abusers are less than 31 years of age, 10 percent are over 50 years of age, and the majority of sexual abusers are men. If the abuser is a stranger, the child will most likely be abused only once, but if the abuser is someone the child knows, it will continue.

GLOSSARY

abuse- *to injure; violate, defile, to do wrong to.*

anal intercourse- *the penetration of the anus by the penis.*

assault-*to attack with great force.*

ejaculate- *the ejection of sperm during intercourse.*

fondle-*to stroke or touch one's body parts.*

incest- *sexual relations between people who are related by blood or as defined by law.*

marital rape- *sexual intercourse with one's wife against her will.*

molest- *to meddle with so as to trouble or hurt; bother.*

oral copulation- *sexual intercourse involving the mouth.*

pedophilic- *a person who uses children for sexual purposes.*

pervert- *a person with variant sexual behavior.*

pornography- *sexually explicit material.*

rape- *a violent sexual crime; sexual intercourse with a person against his\her will.*

rape trauma syndrome- *a group of various symptoms experienced by a rape victim—— fear, self-blame, anxiety, crying, sleeplessness, anger, rage—— that accompany the aftermath of rape.*

rapist- *a person who rapes.*

sex abuse- *to injure sexually.*

sexual intercourse- *penile\vaginal penetration.*

sodomy- *anal intercourse; sex in the rear end.*

statutory rape- *sexual intercourse with a male\female who is under a legally prescribed age.*

torture- *to purposely hurt; great pain, agony.*

victim- *a person who is hurt.*

virgin- *a woman who has never had sexual intercourse.*

virginity- *the condition of being a virgin.*

WORD FROM THE AUTHOR

I had never realized how much I'd been effected mentally after the tragic rapes until I started reading about other peoples' experiences and the inner conflicts it caused. I then looked back on my own life and remembered the fluctuating emotions, unexplainable outbursts and the deep dark depressions that (at the time) seemed to stem from nowhere. At that point I was finally able to start talking about the pain which had been buried in my subconscious causing emotional turmoil for well over a decade. It was such a relief, after all those years to get it out of my system and have back my inner peace. It felt good to know that I was not responsible for the vicious attacks. For a change I was able to place the blame where it belonged.

It is very devastating for anyone to experience the trauma of sexual abuse and even more so when one does find the strength to tell of his\her ordeal only to be doubted and or ridiculed. Many times the impact has a negative effect on the victim without he/she realizing the connection until years later. That's why it's so important to get it out and deal with it. Eventhough we experience misfortunes in life, we don't have to let them hold us back forever. God sent us here to be happy and that's what we all should strive for. I encourage all victims to tell someone if for no reason other than to lift the heavysome burden from within your heart. I further encourage you to seek help whether it's through God, a counselor or any other means you may have to put it into some kind of perspective. It can hold you back and cause tremendous conflict, more than you'll ever realize. Resolve it and go on with your life. If your kids were abused get them help—— immediately!

God bless